0

Contents

Introduction:

THE RAPID EVOLUTION OF AI TECHNOLOGY

The rapid evolution of AI technology has ushered in an era of unprecedented innovation, transforming the way we live, work, and interact with the world around us. From its humble beginnings as a concept in the realm of science fiction, AI has swiftly evolved into a powerful and pervasive force, permeating nearly every facet of modern life.

The initial seeds of AI were sown in the 1950s, with early pioneers such as Alan Turing and John McCarthy laying the groundwork for what would become a revolutionary technological advancement. These visionaries envisioned a future where machines could replicate human intelligence, performing tasks that were once exclusive to human cognition. However, the practical application of AI remained elusive for several decades, constrained by technological limitations and a lack of computational power.

The turning point came in the 21st century, as advancements in computing power, data availability, and algorithmic sophistication propelled AI into the forefront of technological progress. Breakthroughs in machine learning and deep learning algorithms revolutionized the way AI systems processed and analyzed data, enabling them to recognize patterns, make decisions, and perform complex tasks with increasing efficiency and accuracy.

The proliferation of big data further accelerated the evolution of AI, providing the necessary fuel for training sophisticated models and algorithms. With the exponential growth of data sources and the development of scalable computing infrastructures, AI applications began to permeate diverse sectors, ranging from healthcare and finance to transportation and entertainment. AI-driven solutions became integral to enhancing productivity, streamlining operations, and fostering innovation across various industries.

The emergence of neural networks and natural language processing facilitated the development of conversational AI, enabling machines to comprehend and generate human-like language, thereby revolutionizing communication and interaction between humans and machines. This marked a significant leap forward in the quest to create more intuitive and user-friendly AI interfaces, paving the way for the integration of AI-powered virtual assistants and chatbots into everyday life.

Furthermore, the advent of reinforcement learning and generative adversarial networks (GANs) expanded the capabilities of AI systems, empowering them to engage in autonomous decision-making, creative content generation, and problem-solving in dynamic and complex environments. This evolution opened new frontiers for AI applications in fields such as robotics, gaming, art, and design, showcasing the remarkable potential of AI to augment human capabilities and creativity.

As AI continues to evolve at an unprecedented pace, the boundaries of what is achievable are continually being pushed, raising profound questions about the ethical, societal, and philosophical implications of this transformative technology. The rapid evolution of AI technology has not only reshaped our understanding of intelligence but has also redefined the possibilities of what can be achieved in the realms of innovation, productivity, and human progress.

THE IMPACT OF AI ON VARIOUS ASPECTS OF HUMAN LIFE

The impact of AI on various aspects of human life has been profound, ushering in a new era of unprecedented opportunities, challenges, and transformations across numerous domains. From revolutionizing industries to shaping everyday experiences, AI has permeated nearly every facet of modern existence, leaving an indelible mark on society, economy, and culture.

Healthcare: AI has revolutionized healthcare by enabling more accurate diagnoses, personalized treatment plans, and efficient management of patient data. From medical imaging analysis to drug discovery and personalized medicine, AI has accelerated the pace of medical innovation, leading to improved patient outcomes and enhanced healthcare delivery.

Education: AI-powered tools and platforms have transformed the education sector by offering personalized learning experiences, adaptive tutoring, and interactive educational content. AI-driven systems facilitate customized learning paths, promote student engagement, and provide educators with valuable insights for optimizing teaching strategies.

Finance: AI has reshaped the financial industry by streamlining operations, automating processes, and enhancing risk management. From algorithmic trading to fraud detection and customer service, AI-driven solutions have improved efficiency, accuracy, and decision-making in the realm of finance, thereby redefining the landscape of banking and financial services.

Manufacturing: AI has revolutionized manufacturing processes by enabling automation, predictive maintenance, and quality control. AI-powered robotics and smart manufacturing systems have enhanced production efficiency, minimized downtime, and optimized supply chain management, leading to increased productivity and cost-effectiveness in the manufacturing sector.

Transportation: AI has transformed the transportation industry through the development of autonomous vehicles, traffic management systems, and predictive analytics for logistics and supply chain operations. AI-driven innovations have improved safety, efficiency, and sustainability in transportation, paving the way for the realization of smart cities and advanced mobility solutions.

Entertainment: AI has redefined the entertainment landscape by facilitating personalized content recommendations, immersive gaming experiences, and creative content generation. AI-driven algorithms and technologies have enhanced user engagement, content discovery, and storytelling, thereby reshaping the way audiences consume and interact with entertainment media.

Retail: AI has revolutionized the retail sector by enabling personalized shopping experiences, dynamic pricing strategies, and efficient inventory management. AI-powered analytics and recommendation systems have optimized customer engagement, increased sales, and improved overall operational efficiency in the retail industry.

Security and Surveillance: AI has bolstered security and surveillance systems by enabling advanced threat detection, facial recognition, and anomaly detection. AI-driven technologies have enhanced public safety, cybersecurity, and crime prevention, contributing to the development of robust and proactive security measures in various domains.

The impact of AI on these diverse aspects of human life underscores its transformative potential and the need for responsible and ethical deployment to ensure its benefits are maximized while mitigating potential risks and challenges. As AI continues to evolve, its influence will continue to shape the way we live, work, and interact, ultimately redefining the future of human civilization.

A BRIEF HISTORY OF AI DEVELOPMENT AND MILESTONES

The history of AI development is marked by significant milestones and breakthroughs that have shaped the evolution of this transformative field. Beginning with its conceptual origins in the mid-20th century, AI has undergone a series of advancements and setbacks, leading to the development of various subfields and applications. Here is a brief overview of key milestones in the history of AI:

Dartmouth Conference (1956): Considered the birth of AI, the Dartmouth Conference brought together leading researchers, including John McCarthy, Marvin Minsky, and Claude Shannon, to discuss the possibility of creating machines that could simulate human intelligence.

The Logic Theorist (1956): Developed by Allen Newell, J.C. Shaw, and Herbert A. Simon, the Logic Theorist was one of the first AI programs capable of proving mathematical theorems.

General Problem Solver (1957): Developed by Newell and Simon, the General Problem Solver was a program designed to mimic human problem-solving skills and laid the groundwork for problem-solving in AI.

The Perceptron (1958): Frank Rosenblatt developed the perceptron, an early form of a neural network capable of learning and recognizing visual patterns. While limited in its capabilities, the perceptron laid the foundation for future developments in neural networks.

Shakey the Robot (1966): Built at Stanford Research Institute, Shakey was one of the first mobile robots capable of reasoning about its actions. It demonstrated rudimentary capabilities for perception, navigation, and problem-solving.

Expert Systems (1970s-1980s): The development of expert systems, such as MYCIN and Dendral, marked a significant milestone in AI, showcasing the potential for AI to mimic human expertise in specialized domains like medicine and chemistry.

AI Winter (mid-1970s to mid-1980s): Due to high expectations and limited technological capabilities, AI experienced a period of reduced funding and interest, known as the AI winter, which slowed down research and development in the field.

Backpropagation Algorithm (1986): The development of the backpropagation algorithm for training neural networks by David Rumelhart, Geoffrey Hinton, and Ronald Williams revitalized research in neural networks and laid the foundation for modern deep learning.

IBM Deep Blue (1997): Deep Blue, developed by IBM, defeated the reigning world chess champion, Garry Kasparov, marking a significant milestone in AI and demonstrating the potential of AI to tackle complex strategic decision-making tasks.

Introduction of Big Data (2000s): The proliferation of big data and advancements in data storage and processing capabilities provided a wealth of data for training and testing AI algorithms, accelerating the development of machine learning and data-driven AI applications.

Deep Learning Revolution (2010s): Breakthroughs in deep learning, including the development of convolutional neural networks (CNNs) and recurrent neural networks (RNNs), revolutionized AI, leading to significant advancements in image recognition, natural language processing, and other complex tasks.

AlphaGo's Victory (2016): Google's AlphaGo defeated the world champion in the ancient board game Go, showcasing the unprecedented capabilities of AI in mastering complex strategy games and decision-making processes.

Current Developments: AI continues to advance rapidly, with ongoing developments in reinforcement learning, natural language processing, and robotics, among other areas. The integration of AI into various sectors, including healthcare, finance, and transportation, is reshaping industries and transforming the way we live and work.

These milestones in the history of AI highlight the continuous evolution and remarkable progress in the field, laying the foundation for the development of increasingly sophisticated AI systems with diverse applications and implications for society.

CHAPTER 1:

Understanding Artificial Intelligence

Introduction:

Artificial Intelligence (AI) has become a cornerstone of modern technological innovation, shaping the way we interact with machines and revolutionizing various industries. This chapter aims to provide a comprehensive understanding of AI, covering its fundamental concepts, applications, and underlying principles.

Section 1: Defining AI

1.1. Historical Context: Tracing the origins of AI from its conceptual beginnings to its evolution into a dynamic and multifaceted field.

1.2. Core Definitions: Exploring the various definitions of AI, including its broader implications and the distinctions between narrow AI, general AI, and superintelligence.

Section 2: Types of AI

2.1. Narrow AI: Delving into the realm of specialized AI designed for specific tasks and applications, such as image recognition, language translation, and recommendation systems.

2.2. General AI: Exploring the concept of AI systems that can perform any intellectual task that a human being can, showcasing the challenges and possibilities of achieving human-like intelligence in machines.

2.3. Superintelligence: Examining the theoretical potential of AI systems surpassing human intelligence, along with the ethical and existential implications of creating such advanced AI.

Section 3: Fundamental Principles of AI

3.1. Machine Learning: Providing an overview of machine learning algorithms, including supervised learning, unsupervised learning, and reinforcement learning, and their applications in various domains.

3.2. Deep Learning: Exploring the principles of deep learning and neural networks, emphasizing their role in enabling AI systems to process complex data and make sophisticated decisions.

3.3. Natural Language Processing: Investigating the techniques and applications of natural language processing, highlighting its significance in enabling machines to understand and generate human language.

Conclusion:

Summarizing the key concepts and principles discussed in the chapter, emphasizing the transformative potential of AI and its significance in shaping the future of technology and society. This chapter sets the stage for a deeper exploration of AI's impact on various industries and its broader implications for the future of human civilization.

Defining AI and its various subfields

Certainly, defining AI and its various subfields is crucial in comprehending the breadth and depth of this multifaceted field. Below is an outline that can be used as a starting point for this section:

Section 1: Defining AI

1.1. Conceptual Understanding:

- Establishing a comprehensive definition of Artificial Intelligence (AI), encompassing its capacity to imitate cognitive functions such as learning, problem-solving, and decision-making, typically associated with human intelligence.

- Highlighting AI's capacity to perceive its environment, interpret data, and take actions that maximize the chances of achieving specific goals, all while adapting to new inputs and experiences.

1.2. Functional Overview:
- Illustrating the functional scope of AI in replicating human intelligence across various domains, including but not limited to perception, reasoning, learning, problem-solving, and natural language processing.

- Emphasizing AI's ability to handle complex and large datasets, enabling it to identify patterns, make predictions, and generate insights that can inform decision-making processes.

Section 2: Various Subfields of AI

2.1. Machine Learning (ML):
- Defining machine learning as a subset of AI that focuses on the development of algorithms and statistical models, enabling computer systems to improve their performance on a specific task through iterative learning from data.

- Distinguishing between supervised learning, unsupervised learning, and reinforcement learning techniques, highlighting their respective applications and significance in training AI models.

2.2. Natural Language Processing (NLP):
- Describing NLP as a specialized branch of AI that facilitates the interaction between computers and human languages, encompassing tasks such as language translation, sentiment analysis, and text generation.

- Exploring the challenges associated with understanding and processing human language, including semantic analysis, context comprehension, and language generation.

2.3. Computer Vision:

- Introducing computer vision as a subfield of AI that enables machines to interpret and comprehend visual information from images or videos, akin to human visual perception.

- Examining the applications of computer vision in tasks such as image recognition, object detection, facial recognition, and video analysis, elucidating its role in various sectors, including healthcare, automotive, and security.

2.4. Robotics and Autonomous Systems:

- Defining robotics and autonomous systems as the intersection of AI and engineering, focused on designing, developing, and deploying machines capable of performing tasks autonomously or with minimal human intervention.

- Highlighting the integration of AI techniques in robotics to enable machines to perceive their environment, make decisions, and execute actions in real-world scenarios, fostering advancements in fields such as manufacturing, healthcare, and space exploration.

This section serves as a comprehensive introduction to the diverse facets of AI, paving the way for a deeper exploration of each subfield's applications, challenges, and potential future advancements.

Different types of AI (Narrow AI, General AI, Superintelligence)

Understanding the distinctions between different types of AI— Narrow AI, General AI, and Superintelligence—provides valuable insights into the varying degrees of AI capabilities and their implications. Here is an outline that elaborates on each type:

Section: Different Types of AI

Narrow AI:
1.1. Definition:
Introducing Narrow AI as AI that is designed and trained for a specific task or set of tasks, exhibiting expertise within a limited scope of functionalities.

Illustrating how Narrow AI systems excel in performing well-defined tasks, such as language translation, image recognition, and recommendation systems, but lack the ability to generalize their intelligence beyond the designated domain.

1.2. Applications:

Exploring the diverse applications of Narrow AI across industries, including virtual assistants, automated customer service, and predictive analytics, underscoring its role in streamlining processes and enhancing efficiency in specialized tasks.

General AI:
2.1. Definition:
Defining General AI as an advanced form of AI that possesses human-like cognitive abilities, enabling it to understand, learn, and apply knowledge across diverse domains and tasks.

Emphasizing the capacity of General AI to exhibit a broad spectrum of cognitive functions, including reasoning, problem-solving, creativity, and adaptability, akin to human intelligence.

2.2. Challenges and Possibilities:
Addressing the challenges and complexities associated with achieving General AI, such as the development of adaptable learning algorithms, robust decision-making frameworks, and comprehensive knowledge representation.

Discussing the potential implications of General AI for society, including its impact on employment, education, and the nature of human-machine interactions, while highlighting the ethical considerations and risks involved in its development.

Superintelligence:

3.1. Definition:

Introducing Superintelligence as a theoretical concept representing an AI system that surpasses human intelligence across all cognitive abilities and problem-solving capacities.

Exploring the notion of Superintelligence as an entity capable of self-improvement, recursive learning, and unparalleled decision-making capabilities, raising profound existential questions about the control and governance of such advanced AI systems.

3.2. Ethical and Existential Considerations:

Examining the ethical dilemmas and existential risks associated with the development of Superintelligence, including concerns related to AI alignment, value alignment, and the potential for unintended consequences arising from the pursuit of highly autonomous and self-aware AI systems.

Analyzing the necessity of robust ethical frameworks, safety protocols, and regulatory measures to mitigate the risks and ensure the responsible development and deployment of Superintelligence.

This section provides a comprehensive overview of the distinct categories of AI, outlining their capabilities, applications, and implications for society and the future of AI development.

The fundamental principles of machine learning and deep learning

Understanding the fundamental principles of machine learning and deep learning is essential for comprehending the underlying mechanisms that drive AI's ability to process complex data and make informed decisions. Here is an outline that explores these principles in detail:

Section: The Fundamental Principles of Machine Learning and Deep Learning

Machine Learning (ML):

1.1. Definition and Basics:

- Introducing machine learning as a subset of AI that focuses on enabling systems to learn from data, identify patterns, and make decisions without explicit programming.

- Explaining the basic components of machine learning, including data preprocessing, model training, evaluation, and prediction, highlighting the iterative nature of the learning process.

1.2. Types of Machine Learning:

- Distinguishing between supervised learning, unsupervised learning, and reinforcement learning, elucidating their respective methodologies, applications, and underlying algorithms.

- Providing real-world examples of each type to illustrate how they are utilized in various domains, such as image classification, clustering, and autonomous decision-making.

Deep Learning:

2.1. Introduction to Neural Networks:

- Introducing neural networks as the foundation of deep learning, outlining their architecture, layers, and activation functions, and emphasizing their capacity to process complex data and extract high-level abstractions.

- Explaining the role of neurons, weights, and biases in neural networks, illustrating how they enable the system to learn hierarchical representations of data.

2.2. Convolutional Neural Networks (CNNs):

- Exploring the applications of CNNs in image recognition, object detection, and computer vision tasks, showcasing their ability to extract spatial hierarchies and features from visual data.

- Discussing the convolutional, pooling, and fully connected layers within CNNs, highlighting their significance in capturing and processing visual information.

2.3. Recurrent Neural Networks (RNNs):

- Describing the sequential nature of RNNs and their applications in natural language processing, time series analysis, and speech recognition tasks.

- Examining the challenges associated with capturing long-term dependencies and the emergence of advanced architectures like Long Short-Term Memory (LSTM) and Gated Recurrent Unit (GRU) networks to address these challenges.

Training and Optimization:

3.1. Loss Functions and Optimization Algorithms:

- Explaining the role of loss functions in evaluating the performance of machine learning models and deep learning architectures, emphasizing their importance in guiding the optimization process.

- Discussing popular optimization algorithms such as gradient descent, stochastic gradient descent, and their variants, outlining their impact on model convergence and efficiency.

3.2. Regularization and Overfitting:

- Investigating the concepts of regularization and overfitting in the context of model training, highlighting the strategies for mitigating overfitting, including dropout, batch normalization, and early stopping.

- Emphasizing the importance of balancing model complexity and generalization to ensure the robustness and reliability of machine learning and deep learning models.

This section provides a comprehensive exploration of the fundamental principles underlying machine learning and deep learning, setting the stage for a deeper understanding of their applications and implications in various domains.

CHAPTER 2:

AI in Society and Industry

Introduction: The integration of AI into various aspects of society and industry has brought about transformative changes, impacting how we live, work, and interact with technology. This chapter aims to explore the multifaceted implications of AI adoption, emphasizing its role in shaping societal structures and revolutionizing industrial landscapes.

Section 1: AI's Impact on the Workforce

1.1. Automation and Job Displacement:

- Analyzing the effects of AI-driven automation on job markets, industries, and skill requirements, highlighting the potential displacement of certain roles and the emergence of new job opportunities.

- Discussing the need for upskilling and reskilling initiatives to empower the workforce and mitigate the adverse impacts of automation on employment.

1.2. AI-Augmented Work Environments:

- Exploring the concept of human-AI collaboration in the workplace, showcasing how AI tools and technologies can enhance productivity, decision-making, and innovation among employees.

- Examining case studies of organizations integrating AI-driven solutions to streamline operations, optimize workflows, and foster a culture of continuous learning and adaptation.

Section 2: AI's Influence on Healthcare

2.1. Personalized Medicine and Treatment:

- Investigating how AI-powered analytics and predictive modeling are revolutionizing healthcare delivery, enabling personalized diagnosis, treatment plans, and patient care.

- Examining the implications of AI-driven precision medicine in improving patient outcomes, reducing healthcare costs, and advancing medical research and development.

2.2. Diagnostic Imaging and Disease Detection:
- Highlighting the role of AI in diagnostic imaging, including its applications in radiology, pathology, and medical imaging analysis for early disease detection and accurate diagnosis.

- Discussing the challenges and opportunities associated with integrating AI-driven imaging technologies into clinical practices and healthcare systems to improve diagnostic accuracy and patient care.

Section 3: AI's Impact on Education

3.1. Personalized Learning and Adaptive Tutoring:
- Exploring how AI-driven educational platforms and tools can customize learning experiences, cater to individual student needs, and facilitate adaptive tutoring and skill development.

- Discussing the potential of AI in promoting interactive and immersive learning environments that foster critical thinking, creativity, and problem-solving skills among students.

3.2. Education Accessibility and Equity:
- Examining the role of AI in promoting education accessibility and equity, particularly in underserved communities and regions with limited access to traditional educational resources.

- Addressing the challenges and ethical considerations associated with AI integration in educational settings, emphasizing the need for inclusive and responsible AI-driven educational initiatives.

Conclusion: Summarizing the diverse impacts of AI on society and industry, underscoring the need for ethical and inclusive

AI integration to foster sustainable development, equitable opportunities, and societal well-being. This chapter emphasizes the significance of responsible AI adoption in ensuring positive societal transformations and equitable industrial advancements.

The role of AI in transforming various industries (healthcare, finance, manufacturing, etc.)

The role of AI in transforming various industries, including healthcare, finance, manufacturing, and more, is instrumental in driving innovation, enhancing efficiency, and fostering advancements in these sectors. Understanding how AI is reshaping these industries can provide valuable insights into the potential and challenges associated with AI integration. Here is an outline that delves into the transformative role of AI in key industries:

Section: The Role of AI in Transforming Various Industries

Healthcare Industry:

1.1. Personalized Treatment and Care:

- Exploring how AI-driven algorithms and predictive analytics enable personalized treatment plans and patient care, considering individual health data, genetic profiles, and medical history.

- Highlighting the impact of AI-powered precision medicine in improving treatment outcomes, optimizing healthcare delivery, and fostering proactive disease management.

1.2. Medical Imaging and Diagnostics:

- Discussing the integration of AI in medical imaging analysis, including its applications in radiology, pathology, and diagnostic imaging for accurate disease detection and early diagnosis.

- Analyzing the role of AI-driven imaging technologies in enhancing diagnostic accuracy, reducing interpretation errors, and expediting the detection of critical health conditions.

Finance Industry:

2.1. Risk Management and Fraud Detection:

- Examining how AI-powered algorithms and data analytics facilitate proactive risk assessment, fraud detection, and cybersecurity measures in the financial sector, bolstering security and mitigating financial risks.

- Discussing the implications of AI in enhancing regulatory compliance, ensuring data security, and safeguarding financial transactions and customer information.

2.2. Algorithmic Trading and Investment Strategies:

- Analyzing the use of AI in algorithmic trading and investment management, leveraging predictive models and data-driven insights to optimize trading decisions and portfolio diversification.

- Exploring the role of AI-driven investment strategies in facilitating real-time market analysis, portfolio risk assessment, and informed decision-making for financial institutions and investors.

Manufacturing Industry:

3.1. Process Automation and Optimization:

- Illustrating how AI-powered automation and robotics streamline manufacturing processes, enhance production efficiency, and minimize operational costs by automating repetitive tasks and complex workflows.

- Discussing the integration of AI-driven predictive maintenance and quality control systems in optimizing production schedules, reducing downtime, and ensuring product quality and consistency.

3.2. Supply Chain Management and Logistics:

- Examining the role of AI in supply chain management and logistics, enabling efficient inventory management, demand forecasting, and real-time logistics optimization for enhanced operational transparency and cost-effectiveness.

- Analyzing the impact of AI-driven predictive analytics and demand forecasting models in mitigating supply chain disruptions, optimizing resource allocation, and improving overall supply chain performance and resilience.

Retail Industry:

4.1. Customer Engagement and Personalized Experiences:

- Discussing how AI-driven customer analytics and recommendation systems enhance customer engagement, personalize shopping experiences, and facilitate targeted marketing campaigns to optimize sales and customer retention.

- Analyzing the role of AI in predicting consumer behavior, understanding purchase patterns, and delivering tailored product recommendations, driving enhanced customer satisfaction and loyalty.

4.2. Inventory Management and Supply Chain Optimization:

- Exploring the use of AI in inventory management and supply chain optimization, enabling real-time inventory tracking, demand forecasting, and logistics coordination to minimize stockouts and reduce operational costs.

- Discussing the integration of AI-driven supply chain analytics and inventory replenishment models in improving operational efficiency, optimizing product availability, and meeting customer demands in a dynamic retail environment.

This section provides a comprehensive exploration of how AI is reshaping diverse industries, emphasizing its transformative impact on operational efficiency, customer engagement, and strategic decision-making in the modern business landscape.

AI's impact on employment and the workforce

AI's impact on employment and the workforce is a critical topic that requires a comprehensive analysis of the opportunities, challenges, and potential transformations that AI integration brings to the modern labor market. Here is an outline that addresses the multifaceted implications of AI on employment and the workforce:

Section: AI's Impact on Employment and the Workforce

Displacement and Job Transformation:

1.1. Automation and Task Substitution:

- Examining how AI-driven automation and robotic technologies are replacing repetitive and routine tasks across various industries, leading to the potential displacement of certain job roles and responsibilities.

- Discussing the implications of task substitution on workforce dynamics, job requirements, and the need for reskilling and upskilling initiatives to facilitate workforce adaptation to changing job demands.

1.2. Emergence of New Job Roles and Skill Requirements:

- Analyzing the emergence of new job roles and skill requirements resulting from AI integration, emphasizing the demand for specialized AI-related skills, such as data analysis, machine learning, and AI system development, across diverse industries.

- Discussing the importance of fostering a culture of continuous learning and professional development to equip the workforce with the necessary skills and competencies required for the evolving job landscape.

AI-Augmented Work Environments:

2.1. Human-AI Collaboration and Complementarity:

- Exploring the concept of human-AI collaboration in the workplace, emphasizing the synergistic relationship between human capabilities and AI-driven technologies in enhancing productivity, decision-making, and innovation.

- Discussing case studies and best practices illustrating how organizations are leveraging

AI to augment human potential, improve work efficiency, and foster a collaborative work culture that combines human creativity and critical thinking with AI-driven insights and automation.

2.2. Ethical Considerations and Workplace Dynamics:

- Addressing the ethical considerations associated with AI implementation in the workforce, including concerns related to data privacy, algorithmic biases, and the ethical use of AI-driven decision-making systems in employment contexts.

- Highlighting the importance of establishing ethical guidelines, transparent AI governance frameworks, and responsible AI deployment practices to promote a fair and inclusive work environment that upholds ethical values and respects employee rights and well-being.

Reskilling and Upskilling Initiatives:

3.1. Lifelong Learning and Continuous Training Programs:

- Examining the significance of lifelong learning and continuous training programs in empowering employees to adapt to AI-driven workplace transformations, fostering a culture of innovation, and nurturing a skilled workforce capable of thriving in a rapidly evolving job market.

- Discussing the role of educational institutions, businesses, and government initiatives in providing accessible reskilling and upskilling opportunities, promoting workforce agility, and mitigating the adverse impacts of AI-driven job displacements through strategic retraining programs and educational partnerships.

3.2. Collaboration between Industry and Academia:

- Highlighting the importance of fostering collaboration between industry stakeholders and educational institutions to bridge the gap between theoretical knowledge and practical skills required for AI-related job roles and emerging industries.

- Discussing the benefits of industry-academia partnerships in developing AI-focused curriculum, facilitating hands-on training, and promoting industry-relevant research to equip the workforce with the requisite skills and expertise to thrive in AI-driven workplaces and industries.

This section aims to provide a comprehensive understanding of AI's impact on employment and the workforce, emphasizing the need for proactive strategies, ethical considerations, and collaborative efforts to ensure a smooth transition to an AI-integrated job market while fostering a resilient, adaptable, and skilled workforce capable of leveraging the opportunities presented by AI-driven technological advancements.

Societal implications and ethical considerations of AI implementation

Societal implications and ethical considerations of AI implementation are crucial aspects that demand careful examination and responsible decision-making to ensure the equitable and ethical deployment of AI technologies. Here is an outline that explores these implications and considerations in depth:

Section: Societal Implications and Ethical Considerations of AI Implementation

Bias and Fairness in AI Algorithms:

1.1. Algorithmic Bias and Discrimination:

- Examining the presence of biases in AI algorithms and data sets, highlighting the potential consequences of biased decision-making and discriminatory practices perpetuated by AI systems in various domains, including employment, criminal justice, and healthcare.

- Discussing the ethical implications of biased AI algorithms and the importance of implementing fairness-aware AI models, data collection practices, and regulatory frameworks to promote equitable and unbiased decision-making processes.

1.2. Ensuring Diversity and Inclusion in AI Development:

- Analyzing the significance of diversity and inclusion in AI development teams, emphasizing the need for diverse perspectives, experiences, and cultural insights to mitigate biases and foster the creation of AI technologies that are representative, inclusive, and considerate of diverse societal needs and values.

- Discussing the role of ethical guidelines and regulatory measures in promoting diversity and inclusion in AI research, development, and deployment to ensure the equitable and unbiased integration of AI technologies into society.

Privacy and Data Security:

2.1. Data Privacy and Confidentiality:

- Exploring the challenges associated with data privacy and confidentiality in the age of AI, addressing concerns related to the collection, storage, and utilization of personal data by AI systems and algorithms.

- Discussing the importance of robust data protection measures, transparent data handling practices, and informed consent frameworks to safeguard individual privacy rights and prevent unauthorized access or misuse of sensitive personal information by AI-driven technologies.

2.2. Cybersecurity and Ethical Data Usage:

- Highlighting the significance of cybersecurity protocols and ethical data usage policies in AI implementation, emphasizing the need for secure data encryption, network protection, and proactive cybersecurity measures to prevent data breaches, malicious attacks, and unauthorized data manipulation by external threats or malevolent actors.

- Discussing the ethical responsibilities of AI developers, organizations, and policymakers in upholding data security standards, ensuring data transparency, and fostering a culture of responsible data stewardship to build public trust and confidence in AI technologies.

Accountability and Transparency:

3.1. Explainability and Transparency in AI Decision-Making:

- Examining the importance of explainable AI models and transparent decision-making processes, emphasizing the need for AI systems to provide clear explanations, justifications, and insights into their decision-making logic and underlying algorithms to build trust, enhance accountability, and facilitate human understanding and oversight of AI-driven outcomes.

- Discussing the ethical implications of opaque AI systems, black-box algorithms, and the challenges associated with interpreting and auditing complex AI decision-making processes, emphasizing the importance of establishing transparency standards and ethical AI auditing practices to ensure accountability and responsible AI governance.

3.2. Ethical and Legal Frameworks for AI Governance:

- Analyzing the necessity of establishing ethical and legal frameworks for AI governance, encompassing regulatory policies, industry standards, and ethical guidelines that promote responsible AI development, deployment, and usage in alignment with societal values, human rights, and ethical principles.

- Discussing the role of international collaborations, interdisciplinary research, and multi-stakeholder engagement in formulating comprehensive AI governance frameworks, ethical standards, and regulatory guidelines to address the societal implications and ethical challenges of AI implementation in a rapidly evolving technological landscape.

This section aims to provide a comprehensive analysis of the societal implications and ethical considerations surrounding AI implementation, underscoring the significance of ethical AI development, responsible data practices, and transparent governance to ensure the ethical, equitable, and sustainable integration of AI technologies into society.

CHAPTER 3:

Challenges and Limitations of AI

Introduction: While the widespread adoption of AI has brought about transformative advancements across various sectors, the field is not without its challenges and limitations. This chapter aims to delve into the multifaceted obstacles that impede AI progress, examining the technological, ethical, and societal constraints that necessitate careful consideration and strategic solutions.

Section 1: Technical Limitations of AI

1.1. Data Limitations and Quality:

- Investigating the challenges related to data availability, quality, and bias, emphasizing the significance of comprehensive, diverse, and unbiased datasets for training robust and reliable AI models.

- Discussing the implications of limited or poor-quality data on AI performance, accuracy, and generalization, highlighting the need for data preprocessing techniques and data augmentation strategies to address data limitations effectively.

1.2. Computational Constraints and Resource Intensiveness:

- Analyzing the computational demands and resource-intensive nature of AI algorithms, emphasizing the challenges associated with processing large datasets, training complex models, and deploying AI applications in real-time scenarios.

- Discussing the significance of scalable computing infrastructure, cloud-based solutions, and hardware advancements to overcome computational constraints and optimize AI performance in resource-constrained environments.

Section 2: Ethical and Societal Challenges in AI Implementation

2.1. Ethical Dilemmas and Bias Mitigation:

- Examining the ethical dilemmas associated with AI decision-making, algorithmic biases, and discriminatory practices, emphasizing the need for ethical AI frameworks, fairness-aware algorithms, and inclusive AI development practices to mitigate biases and ensure equitable outcomes.

- Discussing the role of interdisciplinary collaborations, diverse stakeholder engagement, and ethical review boards in addressing ethical challenges and fostering responsible AI implementation in diverse societal contexts.

2.2. Socioeconomic Implications and Workforce Displacement:

- Exploring the socioeconomic implications of AI-driven automation, workforce displacement, and skill gaps, highlighting the need for reskilling and upskilling initiatives, job retraining programs, and social safety nets to mitigate the adverse impacts of AI on employment and livelihoods.

- Discussing the significance of inclusive economic policies, universal basic income experiments, and proactive labor market strategies to ensure equitable socioeconomic development and foster a resilient workforce capable of thriving in an AI-integrated economy.

Section 3: Regulatory and Policy Challenges in AI Governance

3.1. Legal Frameworks and AI Governance:

- Analyzing the challenges associated with establishing comprehensive legal frameworks, regulatory policies, and AI governance mechanisms that ensure responsible AI development, deployment, and usage while upholding ethical standards and societal values.

- Discussing the role of international collaborations, regulatory sandboxes, and cross-sectoral partnerships in formulating adaptive and future-proof regulatory frameworks for AI technologies in a rapidly evolving global landscape.

3.2. Privacy Protection and Data Governance:

- Examining the complexities of privacy protection, data governance, and data sovereignty in the context of AI-driven data collection, processing, and utilization, emphasizing the importance of data protection laws, privacy-enhancing technologies, and transparent data handling practices to safeguard individual privacy rights and prevent data misuse or exploitation.

- Discussing the implications of cross-border data flows, data localization policies, and global data governance standards on AI research, development, and cross-border collaborations, emphasizing the need for harmonized international data governance frameworks and privacy regulations to ensure data security and promote global AI innovation.

Conclusion: Summarizing the key challenges and limitations of AI, emphasizing the importance of collaborative problem-solving, interdisciplinary research, and proactive policy interventions to address the multifaceted obstacles and foster a sustainable, ethical, and inclusive AI ecosystem. This chapter underscores the need for holistic approaches and collective efforts to overcome challenges and limitations while harnessing the transformative potential of AI for societal progress and technological innovation.

Addressing biases and ethical dilemmas in AI algorithms

Addressing biases and ethical dilemmas in AI algorithms is crucial to ensuring AI technologies' equitable and responsible deployment. Here is an outline that delves into strategies and approaches for mitigating biases and addressing ethical challenges in AI algorithms:

Section: Addressing Biases and Ethical Dilemmas in AI Algorithms

Identifying Algorithmic Biases

1.1. Data Bias Detection:

- Discussing the methodologies for identifying and assessing biases within training datasets, emphasizing the importance of data preprocessing techniques, data sampling strategies, and diversity-aware data collection practices to mitigate biases and ensure data representativeness.

- Exploring the challenges associated with biased data collection, including historical biases and underrepresented data samples, and the implications of biased data on AI algorithmic performance and decision-making outcomes.

1.2. Bias Detection in Algorithmic Decision-Making:

- Analyzing the methods for detecting biases within AI algorithms and decision-making processes, emphasizing the role of fairness metrics, bias detection tools, and algorithmic audits to identify discriminatory patterns and mitigate biases in AI-driven decision-making systems.

- Discussing the significance of establishing transparent AI governance frameworks, algorithmic accountability measures, and bias mitigation strategies to ensure equitable and unbiased AI outcomes across diverse domains and societal contexts.

Mitigating Algorithmic Biases

2.1. Fairness-Aware AI Algorithms:

- Examining the approaches for developing fairness-aware AI algorithms that prioritize equitable decision-making, emphasizing the implementation of fairness constraints, bias correction mechanisms, and debiasing techniques to ensure AI algorithms do not perpetuate discriminatory practices or reinforce societal biases.

- Discussing the challenges of designing and implementing fairness-aware AI models, including trade-offs between fairness and accuracy, and the need for interdisciplinary collaborations and stakeholder engagements to foster the development of AI technologies that prioritize ethical values and societal well-being.

2.2. Ethical Algorithm Design and Development:

- Emphasizing the importance of integrating ethical considerations into the design and development of AI algorithms, highlighting the significance of ethical AI design principles, inclusive design practices, and ethical review processes to promote responsible AI development and mitigate the risks of biased or discriminatory algorithmic outcomes.

- Discussing the role of interdisciplinary ethics committees, AI ethics boards, and regulatory guidelines in guiding ethical algorithmic design and development, emphasizing the need for proactive ethical decision-making frameworks that prioritize transparency, accountability, and societal welfare in AI technology deployment.

Promoting Ethical AI Governance

3.1. Establishing Ethical AI Standards and Guidelines:

- Exploring the significance of establishing ethical AI standards, guidelines, and best practices that promote transparency, accountability, and ethical decision-making in AI algorithm development and deployment, emphasizing the role of international collaborations, industry partnerships, and regulatory bodies in fostering global AI governance frameworks.

- Discussing the implications of ethical AI standards on AI research, development, and cross-border collaborations, and the need for harmonized international ethical AI regulations that uphold human rights, societal values, and ethical principles in AI technology integration.

3.2. Ethical Education and Awareness Building:

- Highlighting the importance of promoting ethical education and awareness building initiatives that foster a culture of ethical responsibility, data literacy, and AI ethics awareness among AI developers, policymakers, and end-users.

- Discussing the role of educational institutions, industry associations, and public awareness campaigns in promoting ethical AI literacy, fostering ethical decision-making capacities, and nurturing a socially responsible AI ecosystem that prioritizes fairness, transparency, and the protection of individual rights and freedoms.

This section provides a comprehensive overview of strategies and approaches for addressing biases and ethical dilemmas in AI algorithms, emphasizing the importance of proactive measures, ethical governance frameworks, and stakeholder engagements in fostering a culture of responsible AI development and deployment that upholds ethical values and societal welfare.

Exploring the limitations and challenges of current AI technology Top of Form

Exploring the limitations and challenges of current AI technology is crucial for understanding the barriers that hinder the widespread implementation and advancement of AI systems. Here is an outline that delves into the various constraints and challenges facing current AI technology:

Section: Exploring the Limitations and Challenges of Current AI Technology

Data Limitations and Quality Issues

1.1. Data Availability and Accessibility:

- Examining the challenges associated with data availability and accessibility for AI training and model development, emphasizing the implications of limited and unrepresentative datasets on AI performance and generalization.

- Discussing the importance of comprehensive data collection strategies, data sharing initiatives, and data standardization practices to address data limitations and foster the development of robust and reliable AI models.

1.2. Data Quality and Preprocessing Challenges:

- Analyzing the constraints related to data quality and preprocessing requirements for AI algorithms, emphasizing the significance of data cleaning, feature engineering, and data augmentation techniques to improve data quality and enhance AI model training and predictive capabilities.

- Discussing the complexities of data labeling, data annotation, and data verification processes in addressing data quality challenges and ensuring the accuracy and reliability of AI-driven decision-making systems.

Computational Complexity and Resource Intensiveness

2.1. Resource Constraints and Infrastructure Limitations:

- Examining the computational constraints and resource-intensive nature of AI algorithms, emphasizing the challenges associated with scaling AI models, training deep neural networks, and deploying AI applications in resource-constrained environments.

- Discussing the importance of scalable computing infrastructure, cloud-based solutions, and hardware advancements to address computational complexities and optimize AI performance in diverse operational settings.

2.2. Energy Efficiency and Sustainability Concerns:

- Analyzing the energy consumption and sustainability concerns related to AI model training and inference processes, emphasizing the environmental impact of energy-intensive AI computations and the need for energy-efficient AI architectures and algorithms.

- Discussing the role of green AI initiatives, energy-efficient hardware designs, and algorithmic optimizations in promoting sustainable AI development and mitigating the ecological footprint of AI technologies in the era of digital transformation.

Ethical and Regulatory Challenges

3.1. Algorithmic Bias and Fairness Considerations:

- Examining the ethical implications of algorithmic biases and discriminatory AI decision-making outcomes, emphasizing the need for fairness-aware AI models, bias detection tools, and algorithmic audits to ensure equitable and unbiased AI systems.

- Discussing the challenges of addressing algorithmic biases, including the trade-offs between fairness and accuracy, and the importance of interdisciplinary collaborations and ethical governance frameworks in promoting ethical AI development and deployment.

3.2. Privacy Protection and Data Governance:

- Analyzing the complexities of privacy protection and data governance in AI technology deployment, emphasizing the significance of data privacy regulations, transparency policies, and privacy-enhancing technologies to safeguard individual privacy rights and prevent data misuse or exploitation by AI systems.

- Discussing the implications of cross-border data flows, data localization policies, and global data governance standards on AI research, development, and cross-sectoral collaborations, emphasizing the need for harmonized international data governance frameworks and privacy regulations to ensure data security and promote global AI innovation.

This section provides an in-depth exploration of the limitations and challenges facing current AI technology, highlighting the importance of data quality, computational efficiency, ethical considerations, and regulatory compliance in fostering the responsible development and deployment of AI systems that prioritize reliability, transparency, and societal well-being.

The importance of transparency and accountability in AI systems

The importance of transparency and accountability in AI systems cannot be overstated, especially in light of the increasing integration of AI technologies in various domains. Here is an outline that delves into the significance of transparency and accountability in AI systems:

Section: The Importance of Transparency and Accountability in AI Systems

Ensuring Explainability and Interpretability

1.1. Transparent Decision-Making Processes:

- Discussing the significance of transparent decision-making processes in AI systems, emphasizing the need for explainable AI models, interpretable algorithms, and decision-making transparency to facilitate human understanding and oversight of AI-driven outcomes.

- Analyzing the challenges of opaque AI systems and black-box algorithms, and the implications of limited interpretability on AI accountability, human trust, and the ethical deployment of AI technologies in critical domains.

1.2. Human-AI Collaboration and Explainable AI:

- Examining the importance of fostering human-AI collaboration and explainable AI interfaces, emphasizing the role of AI transparency in enhancing user trust, facilitating user control, and promoting meaningful human-AI interactions in various applications and domains.

- Discussing the implications of transparent AI design and development for user experience, user engagement, and the ethical integration of AI technologies that prioritize human-centered design principles and user empowerment.

Promoting Ethical and Responsible AI Deployment

2.1. Algorithmic Accountability and Bias Mitigation:

- Analyzing the significance of algorithmic accountability in mitigating biases and discriminatory practices in AI decision-making, emphasizing the need for bias detection tools, fairness-aware algorithms, and ethical AI auditing practices to ensure equitable and unbiased AI outcomes across diverse societal contexts.

- Discussing the implications of AI accountability for promoting ethical AI deployment, fostering public trust, and safeguarding against algorithmic discrimination and unintended societal biases in AI-driven systems and decision-making processes.

2.2. Regulatory Compliance and Ethical Standards:

- Highlighting the importance of regulatory compliance and ethical standards in AI governance, emphasizing the role of transparent AI governance frameworks, industry guidelines, and regulatory policies in promoting responsible AI development, deployment, and usage.

- Discussing the implications of ethical AI standards on AI research, development, and cross-border collaborations, and the need for harmonized international ethical AI regulations that uphold human rights, societal values, and ethical principles in AI technology integration.

Building Trust and User Confidence

3.1. Trustworthy AI Systems and User Confidence:

- Examining the importance of building trustworthy AI systems that prioritize transparency, accountability, and user privacy, emphasizing the significance of establishing user-centric data handling practices, transparent AI decision-making processes, and ethical data governance frameworks to build user confidence and trust in AI technologies.

- Discussing the implications of transparent AI systems for fostering user engagement, user satisfaction, and long-term user adoption of AI-driven products and services that prioritize data transparency, user privacy, and ethical decision-making practices.

3.2. Stakeholder Engagement and Transparency Policies:

- Highlighting the role of stakeholder engagement and transparency policies in promoting AI transparency, accountability, and responsible innovation, emphasizing the need for transparent communication channels, ethical data-sharing practices, and inclusive AI development processes that prioritize stakeholder input and societal well-being.

- Discussing the implications of transparent stakeholder engagements for fostering collaborative AI development, addressing societal concerns, and promoting a culture of responsible AI innovation that values transparency, accountability, and ethical decision-making.

Chapter 4: The Future of AI

Introduction: The future of AI is marked by unprecedented advancements and transformative potential, with implications spanning various sectors and facets of human life. This chapter delves into the exciting prospects and potential challenges that the future holds for AI, providing insights into emerging trends, transformative applications, and the evolving societal and ethical implications of AI integration.

Section 1: Technological Advancements and AI Evolution

1.1. AI and Quantum Computing:

- Exploring the intersection of AI and quantum computing, discussing the potential for quantum AI to revolutionize computational capabilities, accelerate machine learning processes, and solve complex problems beyond the reach of classical computing.

- Analyzing the challenges and opportunities presented by the fusion of AI and quantum computing, emphasizing its transformative potential for scientific discovery, technological innovation, and the development of advanced AI applications.

1.2. Explainable AI and Ethical Decision-Making:

- Discussing the importance of explainable AI models and ethical decision-making frameworks in promoting AI transparency, fostering trust, and ensuring accountable AI deployment in critical domains such as healthcare, finance, and autonomous systems.

- Analyzing the ethical and societal implications of explainable AI, emphasizing its role in facilitating ethical decision-making, mitigating algorithmic biases, and promoting human-AI collaboration in the future landscape of AI integration.

Section 2: AI and Human-Centric Applications

2.1. Human-Machine Collaboration and Augmentation:

- Examining the evolving dynamics of human-machine collaboration and augmentation, discussing the potential for AI to enhance human capabilities, creativity, and problem-solving skills, fostering a symbiotic relationship between humans and intelligent machines.

- Analyzing the societal implications of AI-augmented human experiences, emphasizing the need for human-centric AI design, inclusive AI development practices, and the preservation of human autonomy and dignity in the future integration of AI technologies.

2.2. Ethical Considerations in Future AI Integration:

- Highlighting the ethical considerations and societal challenges accompanying the future integration of AI into various domains, emphasizing the importance of proactive ethical frameworks, transparent AI governance mechanisms, and stakeholder engagements in shaping the responsible development and deployment of AI technologies.

- Discussing the role of interdisciplinary research, public-private partnerships, and global collaboration in addressing the complex ethical dilemmas posed by the future evolution of AI, ensuring that AI integration aligns with ethical principles, societal values, and human well-being.

Section 3: AI in Emerging Frontiers

3.1. AI in Climate Change Mitigation and Sustainability:

- Exploring the potential applications of AI in addressing climate change, environmental sustainability, and ecological conservation, discussing its role in predictive modeling, data analytics, and the development of sustainable technologies to mitigate the impact of climate change and promote global sustainability.

- Analyzing the challenges and opportunities of AI-driven solutions in the context of climate change adaptation, resource management, and the transition to a sustainable and resilient global ecosystem, emphasizing the transformative potential of AI for fostering a more sustainable and eco-friendly future.

3.2. AI in Space Exploration and Scientific Research:
- Examining the role of AI in advancing space exploration, scientific research, and the exploration of extraterrestrial environments, discussing its potential applications in autonomous space missions, data analysis, and the discovery of new celestial phenomena and planetary systems.

- Discussing the implications of AI-driven space exploration for scientific discovery, technological innovation, and the expansion of human knowledge about the universe, emphasizing its significance in shaping the future of space exploration and our understanding of the cosmos.

Conclusion: Summarizing the promising prospects and potential challenges of the future of AI, emphasizing the need for responsible AI development, proactive ethical frameworks, and collaborative efforts to harness the transformative potential of AI for the betterment of society, scientific progress, and global sustainability. This chapter underscores the importance of ethical AI integration that prioritizes human well-being, environmental conservation, and the advancement of knowledge and innovation for the benefit of humanity and the planet.

Predictions for the future of AI and its potential impact on society

Predictions for the future of AI and its potential impact on society are shaped by the rapid advancements in AI technology and its integration into various sectors. Here is an outline that explores the potential trajectories and societal implications of AI in the future:

Section: Predictions for the Future of AI and Its Potential Impact on Society

AI-Driven Automation and Workforce Transformation

1.1. Job Displacement and Skill Evolution:

- Discussing the potential for AI-driven automation to disrupt traditional job roles and tasks, leading to workforce transformation and the evolution of new job skills and competencies.

- Analyzing the implications of job displacement on the labor market, emphasizing the need for reskilling and upskilling programs to equip the workforce with the necessary skills for the AI-integrated job landscape of the future.

1.2. Human-Machine Collaboration and Work Culture:

- Exploring the potential for AI to augment human capabilities and foster a collaborative work culture that prioritizes human-AI synergy, creativity, and innovation in various industries.

- Analyzing the societal implications of AI-augmented work environments, emphasizing the importance of fostering a human-centered approach to AI integration that values employee well-being, professional development, and the preservation of human autonomy and dignity in the workplace.

51

AI-Enabled Healthcare and Personalized Medicine

2.1. Precision Diagnosis and Treatment:

- Discussing the potential for AI-driven healthcare technologies to revolutionize precision diagnosis, personalized treatment plans, and predictive healthcare analytics, improving patient outcomes and transforming the healthcare landscape.

- Analyzing the societal implications of AI-enabled healthcare advancements, emphasizing the importance of ethical data practices, patient privacy protection, and inclusive healthcare access to ensure equitable healthcare delivery and promote public health initiatives.

2.2. Ethical Considerations and Data Security in Healthcare:

- Highlighting the ethical considerations and data security challenges associated with AI-driven healthcare technologies, emphasizing the need for robust data encryption, secure data sharing protocols, and regulatory compliance to protect patient confidentiality and prevent unauthorized data breaches.

- Discussing the implications of AI-enabled healthcare for patient trust, healthcare equity, and the ethical deployment of AI technologies that prioritize patient-centered care, data transparency, and ethical decision-making processes in the healthcare industry.

AI-Powered Sustainability and Climate Change Mitigation

3.1. Environmental Conservation and Resource Management:

- Exploring the potential for AI to drive sustainability initiatives, promote environmental conservation, and optimize resource management practices for mitigating the impact of climate change and fostering a more sustainable global ecosystem.

- Analyzing the societal implications of AI-driven sustainability solutions, emphasizing the role of AI in promoting eco-friendly technologies, green energy initiatives, and sustainable development practices that prioritize environmental preservation and promote a greener and more sustainable future.

3.2. Ethical AI Governance and Global Collaboration:

- Highlighting the importance of ethical AI governance and global collaboration in addressing complex societal challenges, including climate change, resource depletion, and environmental degradation, emphasizing the role of international partnerships, cross-sectoral collaborations, and ethical AI policies in fostering sustainable development and global environmental conservation.

- Discussing the implications of AI-driven sustainability initiatives for global policy frameworks, sustainable development goals, and the promotion of ethical AI technologies that prioritize environmental stewardship, social responsibility, and the well-being of future generations.

This section provides insights into the potential impact of AI on society, emphasizing the importance of ethical AI governance, stakeholder collaborations, and responsible AI integration to ensure that AI advancements align with societal values, human well-being, and sustainable development goals.

Ethical and regulatory considerations for the future development of AI

Ethical and regulatory considerations for the future development of AI are essential to ensure the responsible and equitable integration of AI technologies into society. Here is an outline that delves into the key ethical and regulatory considerations that should guide the future development of AI:

Section: Ethical and Regulatory Considerations for the Future Development of AI

Ethical Principles and Frameworks for AI Development

1.1. Transparency and Explainability:

- Discussing the importance of transparency and explainability in AI systems, emphasizing the need for clear, interpretable AI decision-making processes and ethical AI design principles that prioritize human understanding and oversight.

- Analyzing the ethical implications of opaque AI systems and black-box algorithms, and the significance of promoting AI transparency to foster trust, accountability, and responsible AI deployment in diverse societal contexts.

1.2. Fairness and Algorithmic Bias Mitigation:

- Highlighting the significance of fairness and algorithmic bias mitigation in AI development, emphasizing the need for fairness-aware AI models, bias detection tools, and ethical AI auditing practices to ensure equitable and unbiased AI outcomes across diverse domains and user groups.

- Discussing the implications of algorithmic biases for societal equality, human rights, and ethical decision-making, and the importance of fostering inclusive AI development practices that prioritize fairness, diversity, and societal well-being.

Regulatory Frameworks and Policy Guidelines for AI Governance

2.1. Legal Compliance and Ethical Standards:

- Examining the challenges and opportunities of establishing comprehensive legal frameworks and ethical standards for AI governance, emphasizing the role of regulatory policies, industry guidelines, and ethical AI certification programs in promoting responsible AI development, deployment, and usage.

- Discussing the implications of AI regulations for cross-border collaborations, data sharing agreements, and global AI innovation, emphasizing the need for harmonized international AI governance frameworks that uphold human rights, societal values, and ethical principles in AI technology integration.

2.2. Data Privacy and Protection Regulations:

- Analyzing the complexities of data privacy and protection regulations in the context of AI-driven data collection, processing, and utilization, emphasizing the importance of data privacy laws, transparent data handling practices, and privacy-enhancing technologies to safeguard individual privacy rights and prevent unauthorized data exploitation by AI systems.

- Discussing the implications of cross-border data flows, data localization policies, and global data governance standards on AI research, development, and cross-sectoral collaborations, emphasizing the need for robust data protection measures and ethical data governance frameworks to ensure data security and promote global AI innovation.

Stakeholder Engagement and Ethical AI Advocacy

3.1. Multi-stakeholder Collaboration and Public Participation:

- Highlighting the significance of multi-stakeholder collaboration and public participation in shaping ethical AI policies and regulatory frameworks, emphasizing the importance of stakeholder consultations, public hearings, and inclusive decision-making processes that foster a culture of responsible AI innovation and governance.

- Discussing the implications of stakeholder engagements for promoting ethical AI advocacy, raising public awareness, and fostering a collaborative AI ecosystem that prioritizes societal values, human rights, and the ethical development of AI technologies.

3.2. Ethical Education and Professional Training:

- Emphasizing the importance of ethical education and professional training programs in fostering a culture of responsible AI development and deployment, highlighting the significance of AI ethics courses, interdisciplinary training workshops, and professional ethics certifications that promote ethical decision-making and AI governance best practices.

- Discussing the implications of ethical education for AI developers, policymakers, and end-users, emphasizing the role of educational institutions, industry associations, and government agencies in promoting AI ethics literacy, fostering ethical decision-making capacities, and nurturing a socially responsible AI workforce that upholds ethical values and societal welfare.

This section provides a comprehensive overview of the ethical and regulatory considerations that should guide the future development of AI, emphasizing the importance of ethical frameworks, transparent governance mechanisms, and stakeholder engagements in fostering a culture of responsible AI development, deployment, and usage that prioritizes societal well-being, human rights, and ethical decision-making practices.

Balancing innovation with responsible AI deployment

Balancing innovation with responsible AI deployment is crucial for fostering sustainable technological advancements that prioritize societal well-being and ethical considerations. Here is an outline that delves into strategies for achieving this balance:

Section: Balancing Innovation with Responsible AI Deployment

Ethical AI Design and Development Principles

1.1. Human-Centric AI Design:

- Discussing the importance of human-centric AI design principles that prioritize user well-being, privacy, and autonomy, emphasizing the significance of inclusive design practices and user-centric feedback loops in fostering responsible AI development.

- Analyzing the implications of human-centered AI design for user engagement, user satisfaction, and the ethical deployment of AI technologies that prioritize user empowerment and societal well-being.

1.2. Ethical AI Development Practices:
- Highlighting the significance of ethical AI development practices that prioritize transparency, accountability, and the protection of individual rights and freedoms, emphasizing the importance of ethical AI guidelines, compliance standards, and ethical review processes in promoting responsible AI innovation.

- Discussing the implications of ethical AI development for fostering user trust, stakeholder confidence, and the adoption of AI technologies that prioritize ethical decision-making and the protection of societal values and norms.

Collaborative Ethical AI Governance

2.1. Multi-Stakeholder Collaboration and Ethical Advocacy:
- Examining the role of multi-stakeholder collaboration and ethical advocacy in promoting responsible AI governance, emphasizing the importance of interdisciplinary partnerships, stakeholder consultations, and public engagement in shaping ethical AI policies and regulatory frameworks.

- Discussing the implications of collaborative AI governance for fostering a culture of responsible innovation, ethical decision-making, and inclusive technological development that prioritizes societal well-being and human rights.

2.2. Regulatory Compliance and Ethical Standards:
- Analyzing the significance of regulatory compliance and ethical standards in guiding responsible AI deployment, emphasizing the role of industry guidelines, ethical AI certification programs, and

regulatory frameworks in promoting AI governance that upholds ethical principles and societal values.

- Discussing the implications of ethical AI standards for fostering industry-wide best practices, promoting ethical decision-making, and ensuring the responsible integration of AI technologies in diverse domains and applications.

Responsible AI Education and Public Awareness

3.1. Ethical AI Literacy and Education:

- Emphasizing the importance of ethical AI literacy and education in fostering a culture of responsible AI deployment, highlighting the role of AI ethics courses, educational workshops, and professional training programs in promoting ethical decision-making and AI governance best practices.

- Discussing the implications of ethical education for AI developers, policymakers, and end-users, emphasizing the need for comprehensive AI ethics training that fosters ethical awareness, critical thinking, and responsible AI development and usage.

3.2. Public Awareness Campaigns and Ethical AI Advocacy:

- Highlighting the role of public awareness campaigns and ethical AI advocacy in promoting responsible AI deployment, emphasizing the significance of transparent communication channels, public forums, and inclusive dialogues that foster public understanding and engagement in ethical AI initiatives.

- Discussing the implications of ethical AI advocacy for fostering a culture of responsible innovation, promoting public trust, and ensuring the ethical integration of AI technologies that prioritize societal

---

welfare and the preservation of human rights and dignity.

This section provides insights into the strategies and approaches for balancing innovation with responsible AI deployment, emphasizing the importance of ethical AI design, collaborative governance, and public awareness initiatives in fostering a culture of responsible AI development that prioritizes ethical values, societal well-being, and the advancement of technological innovation for the benefit of humanity.

CHAPTER 5:

Human-Machine Collaboration

Introduction: Human-machine collaboration represents a paradigm shift in the interaction between humans and intelligent machines, fostering synergistic relationships that leverage the strengths of both entities. This chapter delves into the evolving landscape of human-machine collaboration, exploring the dynamics, challenges, and transformative potential of collaborative interactions between humans and AI-driven systems.

Section 1: Understanding Human-Machine Collaboration

1.1. Cognitive Synergy and Complementary Capabilities:

- Discussing the concept of cognitive synergy in human-machine collaboration, emphasizing the complementary capabilities of humans and AI systems in problem-solving, decision-making, and creative endeavors.

- Analyzing the implications of cognitive synergy for fostering innovative solutions, enhancing productivity, and promoting collaborative intelligence that harnesses the collective strengths of humans and AI technologies.

1.2. User-Centric AI Interfaces and Interaction Models:

- Exploring the significance of user-centric AI interfaces and interaction models in fostering seamless human-machine collaboration, emphasizing the role of intuitive design, natural language processing, and interactive feedback mechanisms in promoting user engagement and satisfaction.

- Analyzing the implications of user-centric AI interfaces for enhancing user experiences, facilitating user control, and fostering meaningful human-AI interactions that prioritize user empowerment and cognitive augmentation.

Section 2: Societal Implications of Human-Machine Collaboration

2.1. Ethical Considerations in Collaborative AI Systems:

- Examining the ethical considerations and societal implications of collaborative AI systems, emphasizing the importance of transparent decision-making, algorithmic accountability, and user privacy protection in fostering responsible human-machine collaboration.

- Discussing the implications of collaborative AI systems for societal trust, ethical decision-making, and the preservation of human autonomy and dignity in the context of AI-driven collaborative endeavors.

2.2. Workforce Transformation and Skill Development:

- Analyzing the implications of human-machine collaboration for workforce transformation and skill development, emphasizing the importance of reskilling and upskilling programs that equip individuals with the necessary competencies for thriving in AI-integrated work environments.

- Discussing the societal implications of workforce transformation for employment opportunities, career development, and the evolution of new job roles that prioritize human-AI collaboration and the cultivation of specialized skill sets for the digital era.

Section 3: Future Prospects of Human-Machine Collaboration

3.1. AI Augmentation and Personalized Experiences:

- Examining the future prospects of AI augmentation in personalized human experiences, discussing the potential for AI-driven personal assistants, cognitive enhancers, and adaptive learning systems that cater to individual preferences and needs.

- Analyzing the implications of AI augmentation for fostering personalized experiences, enhancing user satisfaction, and promoting adaptive human-AI collaboration that prioritizes user well-being, cognitive support, and personalized decision-making processes.

3.2. Collaborative Innovation and Technological Advancements:

- Exploring the role of human-machine collaboration in fostering collaborative innovation and technological advancements, emphasizing the significance of interdisciplinary research, cross-sectoral collaborations, and AI-driven problem-solving approaches in addressing complex societal challenges.

- Discussing the implications of collaborative innovation for technological progress, scientific breakthroughs, and the advancement of knowledge that leverages the collective intelligence of humans and AI technologies for the betterment of society and the planet.

Conclusion: Summarizing the transformative potential and societal implications of human-machine collaboration, emphasizing the need for ethical AI design, user-centric interfaces, and collaborative governance frameworks that foster responsible human-AI interaction and cultivate a culture of innovation, trust, and inclusive technological development for the benefit of humanity and the future of collaborative intelligence.

The importance of fostering collaboration between humans and AI systems

The importance of fostering collaboration between humans and AI systems lies in the transformative potential of leveraging the complementary strengths of human cognition and AI-driven capabilities. Here is an outline that delves into the significance of fostering collaboration between humans and AI systems:

Section: The Importance of Fostering Collaboration between Humans and AI Systems
Harnessing Complementary Strengths for Problem-Solving

1.1. Cognitive Synergy and Collaborative Intelligence:

- Discussing the concept of cognitive synergy and collaborative intelligence in human-AI collaboration, emphasizing the importance of harnessing the complementary strengths of human cognition and AI-driven capabilities in complex problem-solving and decision-making tasks.

- Analyzing the implications of collaborative intelligence for fostering innovative solutions, promoting interdisciplinary research, and addressing complex societal challenges that require diverse perspectives and interdisciplinary approaches.

1.2. Creative Exploration and Innovation:

- Exploring the role of human-AI collaboration in fostering creative exploration and innovation, emphasizing the significance of AI-driven ideation, predictive analytics, and data-driven insights in stimulating creative thinking and breakthrough innovations.

- Analyzing the implications of collaborative innovation for technological progress, scientific discovery, and the advancement of knowledge that leverages the collective intelligence of humans and AI systems for the betterment of society and the exploration of new frontiers in research and development.

Promoting User Empowerment and Cognitive Augmentation

2.1. User-Centric AI Interfaces and Interaction Models:

- Highlighting the importance of user-centric AI interfaces and interaction models that prioritize user empowerment and cognitive augmentation, emphasizing the role of intuitive design, natural language processing, and interactive feedback mechanisms in enhancing user experiences and facilitating meaningful human-AI interactions.

- Discussing the implications of user-centric AI interfaces for promoting user engagement, satisfaction, and cognitive support in diverse domains and applications that prioritize human well-being and the cultivation of a collaborative AI ecosystem.

2.2. Skill Development and Professional Growth:

- Examining the role of human-AI collaboration in skill development and professional growth, emphasizing the importance of reskilling and upskilling programs that equip individuals with the necessary competencies for thriving in AI-integrated work environments and dynamic job landscapes.

- Discussing the societal implications of workforce transformation for employment opportunities, career development, and the evolution of new job roles that prioritize human-AI collaboration and the cultivation of specialized skill sets for the digital era.

Fostering Ethical AI Governance and Responsible Innovation

3.1. Ethical Considerations in Human-AI Collaboration:

- Analyzing the ethical considerations and societal implications of collaborative AI systems, emphasizing the importance of transparent decision-making, algorithmic accountability, and user privacy protection in fostering responsible human-AI collaboration that upholds ethical principles and societal values.

- Discussing the implications of ethical AI governance for promoting user trust, stakeholder confidence, and the adoption of AI technologies that prioritize ethical decision-making and the protection of human rights and dignity.

3.2. Inclusive Collaborative Governance and Public Engagement:

- Highlighting the role of inclusive collaborative governance and public engagement in fostering a culture of responsible AI innovation, emphasizing the significance of stakeholder consultations, public forums, and inclusive dialogues that promote public awareness and participation in shaping the ethical development and deployment of AI technologies.

- Discussing the implications of inclusive collaborative governance for promoting ethical AI advocacy, raising public awareness, and ensuring the responsible integration of AI systems that prioritize societal well-being, human rights, and the advancement of technological innovation for the benefit of humanity and the planet.

This section emphasizes the importance of fostering collaboration between humans and AI systems, highlighting the transformative potential of collaborative intelligence, user empowerment, and responsible innovation that fosters a culture of inclusive technological development and human-AI synergy for the betterment of society and the advancement of knowledge and innovation.

Enhancing human skills through AI augmentation Top of Form

Enhancing human skills through AI augmentation represents a pivotal shift in the interaction between humans and technology, fostering the development of specialized competencies and capabilities that leverage the power of AI-driven systems. Here is an outline that delves into the significance of enhancing human skills through AI augmentation:

Section: Enhancing Human Skills through AI Augmentation

Cognitive Augmentation and Decision-Making Support

1.1. Data-Driven Insights and Cognitive Support:

- Discussing the role of AI-driven data analytics and predictive modeling in providing cognitive support and decision-making insights that enhance human cognitive capabilities and problem-solving skills.

- Analyzing the implications of cognitive augmentation for promoting data-driven decision-making, strategic planning, and informed decision-making processes that leverage AI-generated insights for enhanced human performance and productivity.

1.2. Adaptive Learning and Skill Development:

- Highlighting the significance of AI-driven adaptive learning systems and skill development programs in fostering personalized learning experiences and specialized skill acquisition that cater to individual learning needs and professional development goals.

- Analyzing the implications of adaptive learning for fostering continuous skill enhancement, professional growth, and the evolution of new competencies that align with the demands of the digital era and the dynamic job landscape shaped by AI-driven advancements.

Collaborative Problem-Solving and Innovation

2.1. Interdisciplinary Collaboration and Creative Exploration:

- Exploring the role of AI augmentation in fostering interdisciplinary collaboration and creative exploration, emphasizing the importance of AI-driven ideation, collaborative problem-solving, and the cultivation of innovative solutions that leverage the collective intelligence of humans and AI technologies.

- Analyzing the implications of collaborative innovation for promoting cross-disciplinary research, technological breakthroughs, and the advancement of knowledge that harnesses the cognitive diversity of human expertise and AI-driven insights.

2.2. User-Centric AI Interfaces and Interaction Models:

- Discussing the importance of user-centric AI interfaces and interaction models that prioritize user empowerment and cognitive augmentation, emphasizing the role of intuitive design, natural language processing, and interactive feedback mechanisms in promoting user engagement and cognitive support.

- Analyzing the implications of user-centric AI interfaces for fostering personalized user experiences, enhancing user satisfaction, and promoting adaptive human-AI collaboration that harnesses the collective strengths of human cognition and AI-driven capabilities.

Ethical Considerations and Responsible AI
Deployment

3.1. Algorithmic Accountability and Transparency:

- Examining the ethical considerations and
  societal implications of AI augmentation,
  emphasizing the importance of algorithmic
  accountability, transparency, and user
  privacy protection in fostering responsible AI
  deployment that upholds ethical principles
  and user trust.

- Discussing the implications of ethical AI
  governance for promoting responsible AI
  advocacy, raising public awareness, and
  ensuring the ethical integration of AI
  technologies that prioritize user well-being
  and the protection of human rights and
  dignity.

3.2. Inclusive Collaborative Governance and Stakeholder
Engagement:

- Highlighting the role of inclusive collaborative
  governance and stakeholder engagement in fostering
  a culture of responsible AI innovation, emphasizing
  the significance of interdisciplinary partnerships,
  stakeholder consultations, and public participation in
  shaping the ethical development and deployment of
  AI technologies.

- Discussing the implications of inclusive collaborative
  governance for promoting ethical AI practices,
  regulatory compliance, and the cultivation of a
  collaborative AI ecosystem that prioritizes user
  empowerment, cognitive augmentation, and the
  ethical integration of AI-driven systems for the
  benefit of society and the advancement of human
  potential.

This section underscores the transformative potential of
enhancing human skills through AI augmentation, emphasizing

the importance of cognitive support, collaborative problem-solving, and responsible AI deployment that fosters a culture of inclusive technological development and human-AI synergy for the betterment of society and the cultivation of a skilled workforce equipped to thrive in the digital era.

Ensuring that AI serves human interests and values is critical for fostering a culture of responsible AI development and deployment that prioritizes societal well-being and ethical considerations. Here is an outline that delves into the strategies and approaches for ensuring that AI serves human interests and values:

Section: Ensuring that AI Serves Human Interests and Values

Human-Centric AI Design and Development

1.1. User-Centered Design Principles:

- Discussing the importance of user-centered design principles in AI development, emphasizing the significance of inclusive design practices, user feedback mechanisms, and iterative design processes that prioritize user empowerment and satisfaction.

- Analyzing the implications of user-centric AI design for fostering user trust, engagement, and the adoption of AI technologies that align with human interests, values, and ethical principles.

1.2. Ethical AI Development Practices:

- Highlighting the significance of ethical AI development practices that prioritize transparency, accountability, and the protection of individual rights and freedoms, emphasizing the importance of ethical AI guidelines, compliance standards, and responsible

AI review processes in promoting AI development that serves human interests and values.

- Discussing the implications of ethical AI development for fostering user confidence, stakeholder trust, and the adoption of AI technologies that prioritize ethical decision-making and the protection of human dignity and well-being.

Ethical AI Governance and Regulatory Compliance

2.1. Algorithmic Transparency and Accountability:

- Examining the importance of algorithmic transparency and accountability in AI governance, emphasizing the need for clear decision-making processes, explainable AI models, and ethical AI auditing practices to ensure that AI systems serve human interests and values.

- Discussing the implications of algorithmic transparency for promoting user understanding, algorithmic fairness, and the responsible deployment of AI technologies that prioritize human well-being and societal equity.

2.2. Regulatory Frameworks and Ethical Standards:

- Analyzing the role of regulatory frameworks and ethical standards in guiding responsible AI deployment, emphasizing the importance of industry guidelines, ethical AI certification programs, and governance mechanisms that promote AI integration aligned with human interests, values, and ethical principles.

- Discussing the implications of regulatory compliance for fostering industry-wide best practices, promoting ethical decision-making, and ensuring the responsible integration of AI technologies in diverse domains and applications that serve the greater good of society.

Stakeholder Engagement and Public Advocacy

3.1. Inclusive Collaborative Governance:

- Highlighting the role of inclusive collaborative governance and stakeholder engagement in shaping AI policies and regulatory frameworks, emphasizing the importance of interdisciplinary partnerships, stakeholder consultations, and public participation in ensuring that AI technologies prioritize human interests, values, and societal well-being.

- Discussing the implications of inclusive collaborative governance for promoting ethical AI practices, regulatory compliance, and the cultivation of a collaborative AI ecosystem that serves the needs and aspirations of diverse societal stakeholders.

3.2. Ethical AI Advocacy and Public Awareness:

- Examining the role of ethical AI advocacy and public awareness campaigns in promoting responsible AI deployment, emphasizing the significance of transparent communication channels, public forums, and inclusive dialogues that foster public understanding and engagement in shaping the ethical development and deployment of AI technologies.

- Discussing the implications of ethical AI advocacy for fostering a culture of responsible innovation, promoting public trust, and ensuring that AI technologies serve human interests, values, and the collective well-being of society.

This section emphasizes the importance of fostering AI development and governance that serves human interests and values, highlighting the significance of user-centric design, ethical development practices, and stakeholder engagements that prioritize ethical AI deployment and the advancement of technology for the betterment of humanity and the planet.

Ensuring that AI serves human interests and values

Ensuring that AI serves human interests and values is critical for fostering a culture of responsible AI development and deployment that prioritizes societal well-being and ethical considerations. Here is an outline that delves into the strategies and approaches for ensuring that AI serves human interests and values:

Section: Ensuring that AI Serves Human Interests and Values

Human-Centric AI Design and Development

1.1. User-Centered Design Principles:

- Discussing the importance of user-centered design principles in AI development, emphasizing the significance of inclusive design practices, user feedback mechanisms, and iterative design processes that prioritize user empowerment and satisfaction.

- Analyzing the implications of user-centric AI design for fostering user trust, engagement, and the adoption of AI technologies that align with human interests, values, and ethical principles.

1.2. Ethical AI Development Practices:

- Highlighting the significance of ethical AI development practices that prioritize transparency, accountability, and the protection of individual rights and freedoms, emphasizing the importance of ethical AI guidelines, compliance standards, and responsible

AI review processes in promoting AI development that serves human interests and values.

- Discussing the implications of ethical AI development for fostering user confidence, stakeholder trust, and the adoption of AI technologies that prioritize ethical decision-making and the protection of human dignity and well-being.

Ethical AI Governance and Regulatory Compliance

2.1. Algorithmic Transparency and Accountability:

- Examining the importance of algorithmic transparency and accountability in AI governance, emphasizing the need for clear decision-making processes, explainable AI models, and ethical AI auditing practices to ensure that AI systems serve human interests and values.

- Discussing the implications of algorithmic transparency for promoting user understanding, algorithmic fairness, and the responsible deployment of AI technologies that prioritize human well-being and societal equity.

2.2. Regulatory Frameworks and Ethical Standards:

- Analyzing the role of regulatory frameworks and ethical standards in guiding responsible AI deployment, emphasizing the importance of industry guidelines, ethical AI certification programs, and governance mechanisms that promote AI integration aligned with human interests, values, and ethical principles.

- Discussing the implications of regulatory compliance for fostering industry-wide best practices, promoting ethical decision-making, and ensuring the responsible integration of AI technologies in diverse domains and applications that serve the greater good of society.

Stakeholder Engagement and Public Advocacy

3.1. Inclusive Collaborative Governance:

- Highlighting the role of inclusive collaborative governance and stakeholder engagement in shaping AI policies and regulatory frameworks, emphasizing the importance of interdisciplinary partnerships, stakeholder consultations, and public participation in ensuring that AI technologies prioritize human interests, values, and societal well-being.

- Discussing the implications of inclusive collaborative governance for promoting ethical AI practices, regulatory compliance, and the cultivation of a collaborative AI ecosystem that serves the needs and aspirations of diverse societal stakeholders.

3.2. Ethical AI Advocacy and Public Awareness:

- Examining the role of ethical AI advocacy and public awareness campaigns in promoting responsible AI deployment, emphasizing the significance of transparent communication channels, public forums, and inclusive dialogues that foster public understanding and engagement in shaping the ethical development and deployment of AI technologies.

- Discussing the implications of ethical AI advocacy for fostering a culture of responsible innovation, promoting public trust, and ensuring that AI technologies serve human interests, values, and the collective well-being of society.

This section emphasizes the importance of fostering AI development and governance that serves human interests and values, highlighting the significance of user-centric design, ethical development practices, and stakeholder engagements that prioritize ethical AI deployment and the advancement of technology for the betterment of humanity and the planet.

CHAPTER 6:

Ethical and Legal Frameworks for AI

Introduction: Ethical and legal frameworks for AI serve as essential guidelines and regulations that govern the responsible development, deployment, and usage of AI technologies. This chapter explores the critical aspects of ethical and legal considerations in the context of AI integration, discussing the significance of ethical AI governance, regulatory compliance, and stakeholder collaborations in shaping a robust framework that promotes ethical AI deployment and upholds human values and rights.

Section 1: Ethical Considerations in AI Development and Deployment

1.1. Algorithmic Transparency and Accountability:

- Discussing the importance of algorithmic transparency and accountability in AI development, emphasizing the need for explainable AI models, ethical decision-making processes, and user trust-building measures that promote responsible AI deployment aligned with ethical principles and societal values.

- Analyzing the implications of algorithmic transparency for fostering user understanding, algorithmic fairness, and the ethical integration of AI technologies in diverse applications and domains.

1.2. Fairness and Bias Mitigation:

- Highlighting the significance of fairness and bias mitigation in AI development and deployment, emphasizing the need for fairness-aware AI models, bias detection tools, and ethical AI auditing practices that promote equitable AI outcomes and protect against algorithmic biases that may perpetuate societal inequities and prejudices.

- Discussing the implications of bias mitigation for promoting algorithmic fairness, social justice, and the ethical deployment of AI technologies that prioritize human rights, equality, and the elimination of discriminatory practices in AI-driven decision-making processes.

Section 2: Legal Frameworks and Regulatory Compliance in AI Governance

2.1. Data Privacy and Protection Regulations:

- Examining the role of data privacy and protection regulations in governing AI-driven data collection, processing, and utilization, emphasizing the significance of data privacy laws, transparent data handling practices, and privacy-enhancing technologies that safeguard individual privacy rights and prevent unauthorized data exploitation by AI systems.

- Analyzing the implications of data privacy regulations for promoting user trust, data security, and the responsible integration of AI technologies that prioritize data confidentiality, user consent, and ethical data governance practices.

2.2. Intellectual Property Rights and Ethical AI Development:

- Discussing the importance of intellectual property rights in the context of AI development and innovation, emphasizing the significance of ethical AI patenting practices, responsible technology transfer agreements, and intellectual property protection measures that foster a culture of responsible AI development and ethical innovation.

- Analyzing the implications of intellectual property rights for AI research, industry collaborations, and technological advancements that promote ethical AI development, responsible technology dissemination, and the protection of AI-driven innovations aligned with societal welfare and technological progress.

Section 3: Global Collaboration and Stakeholder Engagement in AI Governance

3.1. International Standards and Collaborative Governance:

- Highlighting the role of international standards and collaborative governance in shaping global AI policies, emphasizing the importance of cross-border collaborations, multilateral agreements, and ethical AI certification programs that promote global AI governance frameworks aligned with human rights, ethical principles, and the advancement of technological innovation for the benefit of humanity.

- Discussing the implications of global collaboration for fostering responsible AI advocacy, ethical technology dissemination, and the cultivation of a collaborative AI ecosystem that prioritizes the collective well-being of society and the planet.

3.2. Stakeholder Engagement and Public Participation:

- Examining the significance of stakeholder engagement and public participation in shaping AI policies and regulatory frameworks, emphasizing the importance of inclusive decision-making processes, stakeholder consultations, and public forums that foster public awareness and engagement in the ethical development and deployment of AI technologies.

- Analyzing the implications of inclusive stakeholder engagement for promoting ethical AI practices, regulatory compliance, and the cultivation of an AI governance framework that serves the needs and aspirations of diverse societal stakeholders, fostering a culture of responsible innovation and ethical technology integration.

Conclusion: Summarizing the key insights into ethical and legal frameworks for AI, emphasizing the importance of algorithmic transparency, regulatory compliance, and stakeholder collaborations in fostering a culture of responsible AI development and governance that prioritizes ethical principles, human rights, and the societal well-being of current and future generations

The need for ethical guidelines in AI development and deployment

The need for ethical guidelines in AI development and deployment is paramount for ensuring the responsible integration of AI technologies that align with societal values, human rights, and ethical principles. Here is an outline that delves into the significance of ethical guidelines in AI development and deployment:

Section: The Need for Ethical Guidelines in AI Development and Deployment

Ensuring Transparency and Accountability

1.1. Algorithmic Transparency and Explainability:

- Discussing the importance of algorithmic transparency and explainability in AI systems, emphasizing the need for clear decision-making processes, interpretable AI models, and ethical AI auditing practices that promote responsible AI deployment aligned with ethical principles and user trust.

- Analyzing the implications of algorithmic transparency for fostering user understanding, algorithmic fairness, and the ethical integration of AI technologies in diverse applications and domains.

1.2. Ethical Decision-Making and Accountability Measures:

- Highlighting the significance of ethical decision-making and accountability measures in AI development and deployment, emphasizing the importance of ethical AI guidelines, compliance standards, and responsible AI review processes that promote AI technologies aligned with ethical principles and human values.

- Discussing the implications of ethical decision-making for fostering user confidence, stakeholder trust, and the adoption of AI technologies that prioritize the protection of human rights and dignity.

Mitigating Bias and Ensuring Fairness

2.1. Fairness-Aware AI Development Practices:

- Examining the role of fairness-aware AI development practices in mitigating biases and ensuring equitable AI outcomes, emphasizing the need for bias detection tools, inclusive data sets, and ethical AI auditing mechanisms that promote algorithmic fairness and protect against discriminatory practices in AI-driven decision-making processes.

- Analyzing the implications of bias mitigation for promoting social justice, algorithmic accountability, and the ethical deployment of AI technologies that prioritize human rights, equality, and the elimination of discriminatory biases.

2.2. Diversity and Inclusion in AI Development:

- Discussing the importance of diversity and inclusion in AI development teams and data collection processes, emphasizing the significance of diverse perspectives, interdisciplinary collaborations, and inclusive AI research practices that promote the development of AI technologies that cater to the needs and aspirations of diverse user groups.

- Analyzing the implications of diversity and inclusion for fostering user-centric AI solutions, promoting societal inclusivity, and ensuring that AI technologies serve the greater good of society and uphold the values of fairness, equity, and diversity.

Upholding User Privacy and Data Security

3.1. Data Privacy Protection and Ethical Data Handling:

- Highlighting the role of data privacy protection and ethical data handling practices in AI development and deployment, emphasizing the importance of data privacy laws, transparent data collection processes, and privacy-enhancing technologies that safeguard individual privacy rights and prevent unauthorized data exploitation by AI systems.

- Analyzing the implications of data privacy protection for promoting user trust, data security, and the responsible integration of AI technologies that prioritize data confidentiality, user consent, and ethical data governance practices.

3.2. Secure AI Systems and Responsible Data Governance:

- Examining the significance of secure AI systems and responsible data governance measures in ensuring the ethical deployment of AI technologies, emphasizing the role of data encryption, secure data sharing protocols, and regulatory compliance in protecting user privacy and preventing unauthorized data breaches in AI-driven systems.

- Discussing the implications of responsible data governance for fostering user confidence, data transparency, and the cultivation of a trustworthy AI ecosystem that prioritizes user privacy, data security, and the ethical use of data for the advancement of technology and the betterment of society.

This section emphasizes the critical need for ethical guidelines in AI development and deployment, highlighting the importance of algorithmic transparency, fairness, user privacy protection, and responsible data governance in fostering a culture of responsible AI innovation and technology integration that upholds ethical principles, human rights, and societal values.

Legal considerations and regulations for AI technology

Legal considerations and regulations for AI technology play a crucial role in ensuring the responsible development, deployment, and usage of AI-driven systems, safeguarding user rights, privacy, and data security. Here is an outline that delves into the legal considerations and regulations for AI technology:

Section: Legal Considerations and Regulations for AI Technology
Data Privacy and Protection Regulations
1.1. Compliance with Data Privacy Laws:
- Discussing the importance of compliance with data privacy laws and regulations in AI technology development and deployment, emphasizing the significance of transparent data handling practices, user consent mechanisms, and privacy-enhancing technologies that safeguard individual privacy rights and prevent unauthorized data exploitation by AI systems.

- Analyzing the implications of data privacy regulations for promoting user trust, data security, and the responsible integration of AI technologies that prioritize data confidentiality, user consent, and ethical data governance practices.

1.2. Cross-Border Data Transfer and Privacy Compliance:

- Highlighting the challenges and opportunities of cross-border data transfer in the context of AI technology, emphasizing the role of international data protection agreements, data localization requirements, and global privacy regulations that govern the cross-border flow of data and promote ethical data governance practices in AI-driven systems.

- Analyzing the implications of cross-border data transfer for global AI research, industry collaborations, and technological advancements, emphasizing the need for legal frameworks that uphold data privacy, user consent, and the protection of sensitive information in the digital era.

Intellectual Property Rights and Patents

2.1. Patent Protection for AI-Driven Innovations:

- Examining the role of patent protection in fostering AI-driven innovations and technological advancements, emphasizing the significance of intellectual property rights, patent applications, and technology licensing agreements that promote responsible technology dissemination and the protection of AI-driven inventions aligned with ethical principles and societal welfare.

- Analyzing the implications of patent protection for AI research, industry collaborations, and the advancement of knowledge, emphasizing the need for legal frameworks that safeguard intellectual property rights, encourage innovation, and foster a culture of responsible AI development and technology integration.

2.2. Ethical AI Patenting Practices and Technology Transfer:

- Discussing the importance of ethical AI patenting practices and responsible technology transfer agreements in AI research and development, emphasizing the significance of ethical AI guidelines, technology sharing protocols, and intellectual property licensing models that promote the ethical dissemination of AI-driven innovations and foster a culture of responsible AI technology integration.

- Analyzing the implications of ethical AI patenting practices for industry partnerships, technology collaborations, and the global dissemination of AI-driven solutions that prioritize user interests, ethical principles, and the collective well-being of society.

Liability and Accountability in AI-Driven Systems
3.1. Legal Frameworks for Algorithmic Accountability:

- Highlighting the role of legal frameworks for algorithmic accountability in governing AI-driven decision-making processes, emphasizing the need for clear liability standards, regulatory compliance measures, and ethical AI auditing practices that promote algorithmic transparency and protect against the risks of algorithmic biases and discriminatory practices in AI systems.

- Analyzing the implications of algorithmic accountability for user rights, consumer protection, and the responsible deployment of AI technologies that prioritize ethical

decision-making, fairness, and the protection
of individual freedoms and human dignity.

3.2. Product Liability and Ethical AI Governance:

- Examining the significance of product liability and ethical AI governance in ensuring the responsible deployment of AI-driven systems, emphasizing the role of product liability laws, regulatory guidelines, and ethical AI certification programs that promote user safety, product reliability, and the ethical use of AI technologies for the benefit of society and the advancement of technology.

- Discussing the implications of product liability for AI manufacturers, service providers, and technology developers, emphasizing the need for legal frameworks that prioritize user safety, ethical decision-making, and the protection of user interests in the development and deployment of AI-driven products and services.

This section provides insights into the legal considerations and regulations for AI technology, emphasizing the importance of data privacy protection, intellectual property rights, liability standards, and ethical AI governance that foster a culture of responsible AI development and deployment, upholding user rights, privacy, and ethical principles in the integration of AI-driven systems for the betterment of society and the advancement of technology.

International perspectives on AI governance and policies

International perspectives on AI governance and policies reflect the global efforts to establish comprehensive frameworks that promote responsible AI development, ethical deployment, and international collaboration in the field of artificial intelligence. Here is an outline that delves into the international perspectives on AI governance and policies:

Section: International Perspectives on AI Governance and Policies

Collaborative Global Initiatives for AI Governance

1.1. Multilateral Agreements and Collaborative Partnerships:

- Discussing the significance of multilateral agreements and collaborative partnerships in shaping international AI governance frameworks, emphasizing the role of intergovernmental organizations, global AI research consortia, and cross-border collaborations that foster the exchange of best practices, regulatory standards, and ethical guidelines for the responsible development and deployment of AI technologies.

- Analyzing the implications of collaborative global initiatives for AI research, industry partnerships, and the cultivation of a global AI ecosystem that prioritizes user interests, human rights, and the advancement of technology for the collective well-being of humanity and the planet.

1.2. International Standards for Ethical AI Development:

- Examining the role of international standards for ethical AI development in fostering global AI governance, emphasizing the importance of ethical AI guidelines, compliance frameworks, and certification programs that promote ethical AI practices, algorithmic transparency, and user privacy protection in AI-driven systems deployed across diverse geographical regions and cultural contexts.

- Analyzing the implications of international standards for ethical AI development for promoting cross-border AI collaborations, technology transfer agreements, and the global dissemination of AI-driven innovations that uphold ethical principles, human values, and the preservation of human dignity and rights.

Ethical AI Governance and Regulatory Compliance

2.1. Cross-Border Data Privacy and Protection Agreements:

- Highlighting the challenges and opportunities of cross-border data privacy and protection agreements in the context of AI governance, emphasizing the role of global data protection regulations, privacy-enhancing technologies, and data localization requirements that safeguard user privacy rights and prevent unauthorized data exploitation in AI-driven systems deployed across international borders.

- Analyzing the implications of cross-border data privacy agreements for promoting user trust, data security, and the responsible integration of AI technologies that prioritize data confidentiality, user consent, and the ethical use of data for the advancement of technology and the betterment of society.

2.2. International Collaboration in AI Research and Development:

- Discussing the importance of international collaboration in AI research and development, emphasizing the significance of cross-border research partnerships, knowledge exchange programs, and collaborative funding initiatives that foster global AI innovations, technological breakthroughs, and the advancement of knowledge in diverse AI domains and applications.

- ·Analyzing the implications of international collaboration for AI researchers, industry stakeholders, and policymakers, emphasizing the need for inclusive research practices, interdisciplinary partnerships, and global knowledge sharing that promote the responsible development and deployment of AI technologies aligned with ethical principles and the societal well-being of humanity.

Global Perspectives on AI Ethics and Human Rights

3.1. Human-Centric AI Design and User Empowerment:

- Examining the significance of human-centric AI design and user empowerment in global AI governance, emphasizing the importance of user feedback mechanisms, inclusive design practices, and user-centric AI interfaces that prioritize user engagement, satisfaction, and the protection of individual rights and freedoms in AI-driven systems deployed across international borders and cultural contexts.

- Analyzing the implications of human-centric AI design for fostering global user trust, stakeholder engagement, and the adoption of AI technologies that prioritize user empowerment, cognitive support, and the ethical integration of AI systems for the benefit of humanity and the advancement of technology.

3.2. Ethical AI Advocacy and Global Stakeholder Engagement:

- Highlighting the role of ethical AI advocacy and global stakeholder engagement in promoting responsible AI governance, emphasizing the significance of inclusive decision-making processes, stakeholder consultations, and public forums that foster global awareness and participation in shaping the ethical development and deployment of AI technologies that uphold human rights, ethical principles, and the preservation of human dignity.

- Analyzing the implications of ethical AI advocacy for fostering a culture of responsible innovation, global AI leadership, and the cultivation of a collaborative AI ecosystem that prioritizes the collective well-being of society and the planet, fostering a global AI governance framework that serves the needs and aspirations of diverse global stakeholders.

This section provides insights into the international perspectives on AI governance and policies, emphasizing the significance of collaborative global initiatives, ethical AI governance, and global perspectives on AI ethics and human rights that foster a culture of responsible AI development, international collaboration, and the advancement of technology for the benefit of global society and the planet.

CONCLUSION:

Reflecting on the transformative power of AI in the modern world illuminates the profound impact of artificial intelligence across diverse sectors, fostering unprecedented technological advancements, societal changes, and economic transformations. Here is an outline that delves into the transformative power of AI in the modern world:

Section: Reflecting on the Transformative Power of AI in the Modern World
AI-Driven Technological Advancements
1.1. Automation and Process Optimization:
- Discussing the transformative power of AI-driven automation and process optimization,

emphasizing the significance of AI technologies in streamlining operations, improving efficiency, and enhancing productivity in various industries, including manufacturing, logistics, and supply chain management.

- Analyzing the implications of AI-driven automation for cost reduction, resource optimization, and the acceleration of business processes that foster innovation, scalability, and competitive advantage in the modern global marketplace.

1.2. Predictive Analytics and Data-Driven Insights:

- Highlighting the transformative power of predictive analytics and data-driven insights in AI applications, emphasizing the role of AI technologies in generating actionable business intelligence, predictive forecasting models, and personalized recommendations that empower decision-makers to make informed choices and drive strategic growth in dynamic market environments.

- Analyzing the implications of predictive analytics for enhancing customer experiences, market segmentation, and the development of targeted marketing strategies that cater to individual preferences, behaviors, and evolving consumer trends in the modern digital era.

Societal Implications and Human-Centric Innovations
2.1. AI-Assisted Healthcare and Medical Breakthroughs:

- Examining the transformative power of AI-assisted healthcare and medical breakthroughs, emphasizing the significance of AI-driven diagnostic tools, personalized treatment plans, and precision medicine approaches that revolutionize disease management, patient care, and the advancement of medical research and clinical trials.

- Analyzing the implications of AI-driven healthcare for enhancing patient outcomes, reducing medical errors, and promoting preventive care strategies that prioritize patient well-being, healthcare accessibility, and the equitable distribution of healthcare resources in the modern healthcare landscape.

2.2. Education and Lifelong Learning Opportunities:

- Discussing the transformative power of AI in education and lifelong learning opportunities, emphasizing the role of AI-driven adaptive learning systems, personalized tutoring platforms, and interactive educational resources that cater to diverse learning styles, foster skill development, and empower learners to thrive in the modern knowledge-based economy.

- Analyzing the implications of AI-driven education for promoting inclusive learning environments, educational equity, and the cultivation of specialized skill sets that align with the demands of the digital era and the evolving job market shaped by AI-driven advancements and technological disruptions.

Ethical Considerations and Responsible AI Integration

3.1. Ethical AI Design and User Privacy Protection:

- Examining the transformative power of ethical AI design and user privacy protection, emphasizing the importance of user-centric AI interfaces, transparent data handling practices, and user empowerment mechanisms that prioritize user privacy, data security, and the protection of individual rights and freedoms in AI-driven systems deployed across various domains and applications.

- Analyzing the implications of ethical AI design for fostering user trust, stakeholder confidence, and the adoption of AI technologies that prioritize ethical decision-making, algorithmic fairness, and the preservation of human dignity and well-being in the modern digital ecosystem.

3.2. Collaborative Governance and Inclusive AI Advocacy:

- Highlighting the role of collaborative governance and inclusive AI advocacy in promoting responsible AI integration, emphasizing the significance of stakeholder consultations, public forums, and inclusive dialogues that foster public awareness and engagement in shaping the ethical development and deployment of AI technologies that serve the greater good of society and uphold the values of fairness, equity, and transparency.

- Analyzing the implications of inclusive AI advocacy for fostering a culture of responsible innovation, global AI leadership, and the cultivation of a collaborative AI ecosystem that prioritizes the collective well-being of humanity and the sustainable advancement of technology for the betterment of society and the planet in the modern interconnected world.

This section reflects on the transformative power of AI in the modern world, highlighting the profound impact of AI-driven technological advancements, societal changes, and ethical considerations that shape the future of AI integration and the role of artificial intelligence in fostering a sustainable, inclusive, and technology-driven society.

Emphasizing the importance of responsible AI development and implementation underscores the critical role of ethical considerations, regulatory compliance, and stakeholder collaborations in fostering a culture of responsible innovation, user trust, and societal well-being in the integration of AI technologies. Here is an outline that delves into the importance of responsible AI development and implementation:

Section: Emphasizing the Importance of Responsible AI Development and Implementation

Ethical Considerations in AI Development

1.1. Algorithmic Transparency and Explainability:

- Discussing the importance of algorithmic transparency and explainability in AI systems, emphasizing the need for clear decision-making processes, interpretable AI models, and ethical AI auditing practices that promote responsible AI deployment aligned with ethical principles and user trust.

- Analyzing the implications of algorithmic transparency for fostering user understanding, algorithmic fairness, and the ethical integration of AI technologies in diverse applications and domains.

1.2. Fairness and Bias Mitigation:

- Highlighting the significance of fairness and bias mitigation in AI development and deployment, emphasizing the need for fairness-aware AI models, bias detection tools, and ethical AI auditing practices that promote equitable AI outcomes and protect against algorithmic biases that may perpetuate societal inequities and prejudices.

- Discussing the implications of bias mitigation for promoting algorithmic fairness, social justice, and the ethical deployment of AI technologies that prioritize human rights, equality, and the elimination of discriminatory practices in AI-driven decision-making processes.

Regulatory Compliance and Accountability

2.1. Data Privacy and Protection Regulations:

- Examining the role of data privacy and protection regulations in governing AI-driven data collection, processing, and utilization, emphasizing the significance of data privacy laws, transparent data handling practices, and privacy-enhancing technologies that safeguard individual privacy rights and prevent unauthorized data exploitation by AI systems.

- Analyzing the implications of data privacy regulations for promoting user trust, data security, and the responsible integration of AI technologies that prioritize data confidentiality, user consent, and ethical data governance practices.

2.2. Ethical AI Governance and Accountability Measures:

- Discussing the importance of ethical AI governance and accountability measures in ensuring responsible AI deployment, emphasizing the role of ethical AI guidelines, compliance standards, and responsible AI review processes that promote AI technologies aligned with ethical principles and human values.

- Analyzing the implications of ethical AI governance for fostering user confidence, stakeholder trust, and the adoption of AI technologies that prioritize the protection of human rights and dignity.

Stakeholder Collaborations and Inclusive Decision-Making

3.1. Inclusive Collaborative Governance:

- Highlighting the role of inclusive collaborative governance in shaping AI policies and regulatory frameworks, emphasizing the importance of interdisciplinary partnerships, stakeholder consultations, and public participation in ensuring that AI technologies prioritize human interests, values, and societal well-being.

- Analyzing the implications of inclusive collaborative governance for promoting ethical AI practices, regulatory compliance, and the cultivation of an AI governance framework that serves the needs and aspirations of diverse societal stakeholders.

3.2. Responsible AI Advocacy and Public Awareness:

- Examining the significance of responsible AI advocacy and public awareness campaigns in promoting ethical AI deployment, emphasizing the role of transparent communication channels, public forums, and inclusive dialogues that foster public understanding and engagement in shaping the ethical development and deployment of AI technologies.

- Analyzing the implications of responsible AI advocacy for fostering a culture of responsible innovation, promoting public trust, and ensuring that AI technologies serve human interests, values, and the collective well-being of society.

This section emphasizes the critical importance of responsible AI development and implementation, highlighting the significance of ethical considerations, regulatory compliance, and stakeholder collaborations that foster a culture of responsible innovation, user trust, and the societal well-being in the integration of AI technologies for the benefit of humanity and the sustainable advancement of technology.

Envisioning a future where AI contributes to the betterment of society illuminates the transformative potential of artificial intelligence in addressing societal challenges, fostering sustainable development, and promoting human well-being. Here is an outline that delves into the vision of a future where AI contributes to the betterment of society:

Section: Envisioning a Future Where AI Contributes to the Betterment of Society

AI-Driven Societal Solutions and Sustainable Development

1.1. AI-Assisted Healthcare and Medical Advancements:

- Discussing the transformative potential of AI-assisted healthcare and medical advancements, emphasizing the role of AI technologies in disease prevention, early diagnosis, and personalized treatment plans that improve patient outcomes, reduce healthcare costs, and foster a healthier society.

- Analyzing the implications of AI-driven healthcare for promoting equitable access to quality healthcare services, enhancing medical research, and advancing public health initiatives that prioritize preventive care, patient well-being, and the sustainability of healthcare systems in the future.

1.2. Environmental Sustainability and Climate Action:

- Highlighting the role of AI in environmental sustainability and climate action, emphasizing the significance of AI-driven data analytics, predictive modeling, and sustainable resource management solutions that empower policymakers, businesses, and communities to make informed decisions and implement effective strategies for mitigating climate change, preserving natural resources, and fostering ecological balance.

- Analyzing the implications of AI-driven environmental sustainability initiatives for promoting global climate resilience, renewable energy adoption, and the implementation of sustainable development goals that prioritize environmental stewardship and the well-being of present and future generations.

AI-Enhanced Education and Empowerment

2.1. Personalized Learning and Skill Development:

- Examining the transformative potential of AI-enhanced education and personalized learning, emphasizing the role of AI-driven adaptive learning platforms, interactive educational resources, and virtual learning environments that cater to diverse learning styles, foster skill development, and empower individuals to acquire the knowledge and skills needed to thrive in the future digital economy.

- Analyzing the implications of AI-driven education for promoting lifelong learning, educational equity, and the cultivation of critical thinking, creativity, and digital literacy skills that prepare individuals for the challenges and opportunities of the future workforce shaped by technological advancements and AI-driven disruptions.

2.2. Inclusive Access to Education and Knowledge Sharing:

- Discussing the significance of AI in fostering inclusive access to education and knowledge sharing, emphasizing the role of AI-driven educational technologies, open educational resources, and digital learning platforms that bridge the digital divide, promote educational equity, and enable individuals from diverse backgrounds and underserved communities to access quality educational opportunities and participate in the global knowledge economy.

- Analyzing the implications of inclusive AI-driven education for promoting social mobility, economic empowerment, and the democratization of knowledge that empowers individuals to become lifelong learners, critical thinkers, and active contributors to the betterment of society and the advancement of human civilization.

Ethical AI Governance and Human-Centric Innovations

3.1. Collaborative AI Governance and Inclusive Decision-Making:

- Highlighting the role of collaborative AI governance and inclusive decision-making in shaping a future where AI serves the greater good of society, emphasizing the importance of stakeholder consultations, interdisciplinary partnerships, and public participation in the development and deployment of AI technologies that prioritize human interests, values, and ethical principles.

- Analyzing the implications of inclusive AI governance for fostering responsible AI innovations, global AI leadership, and the cultivation of an AI ecosystem that promotes the well-being of humanity, upholds human rights, and advances the sustainable development goals for a better and more equitable future.

3.2. Ethical AI Advocacy and User Empowerment:

- Examining the significance of ethical AI advocacy and user empowerment in shaping a future where AI technologies serve human interests and values, emphasizing the importance of transparent communication channels, user-centric design principles, and user privacy protection mechanisms that prioritize user empowerment, trust, and the protection of individual rights and freedoms in AI-driven systems deployed across various societal domains and applications.

- Analyzing the implications of ethical AI advocacy for fostering a culture of responsible innovation, global AI citizenship, and the cultivation of a collaborative AI ecosystem that prioritizes the collective well-being of society, human dignity, and the sustainable advancement of technology for the benefit of present and future generations.

This section envisions a future where AI contributes to the betterment of society, highlighting the transformative potential of AI-driven societal solutions, education empowerment, and ethical AI governance that foster a sustainable, inclusive, and technology-driven society, advancing the well-being of humanity and the preservation of the planet for future generations.

Your Notes

Your Notes

Your Notes

Your Notes

Your Notes

Your Notes

Your Notes

www.ingramcontent.com/pod-product-compliance
Lightning Source LLC
LaVergne TN
LVHW081700050326
832903LV00026B/1844